¿Cómo Hacer Preguntas?

or

How To Make Questions

69 Instructional Poems in English

¿Cómo Hacer Preguntas?

or

How To Make Questions

69 Instructional Poems in English

Daniel Hales

Frayed Edge Press
Philadelphia, PA
2020

Copyright 2020 Daniel Hales

Published by Frayed Edge Press in 2020

Frayed Edge Press
PO Box 13465
Philadelphia, PA 19101

http://frayededgepress.com

Cover images and design by Daniel Hales.

Publisher's Cataloging-in-Publication

Names: Hales, Daniel.
Title: ¿Cómo hacer preguntas? or how to make questions: 69 instructional poems in English / Daniel Hales.
Description: Philadelphia, PA : Frayed Edge Press, 2020.
Identifiers: LCCN 2020935905 | ISBN 9781642510218 (pbk.) | ISBN 9781642510225 (ebook)
Subjects: LCSH: Questions and answers--Poetry. | Uncertainty--Poetry. | BISAC: POETRY / American / General. | POETRY / Subjects & Themes / General.
Classification: LCC PS3608.A447 C66 2020| DDC 811 H35--dc23
LC record available at https://lccn.loc.gov/2020935905

How To Find The Poem You're Looking For

How To Make Questions   3

      ? **Comment Faire La Lumière**
          or
    How To Make The Light Come   ¿

How To Change Your Mind	6-7
How To Deliver A Toast	8-9
How To Hover Above Yourself	10
How To Protect Your Home	11-12
How To Give It A Name	13
How To Paint A Still Life	14
How To Watch A Summer Sunset	15
How To Play Spin The Bottle	16
How To Sing And Why	17
How To Measure The Dew Point	18
How To Define Perpetual	19
How To Get Their Attention	20
How To Describe Iridescence	21
How To Find A Missing Cat	22-23
How To Make The Light Come	24
How To Make Friends	25-26
How To Transform Base Matter Into Gold	27-28
How To Observe Daylight Savings Time	29
How To Pass The Time	30
How To Write A Cover Letter	31
How To Reach Enlightenment	32
How To Complete Your Apprenticeship	33
How To Light A Torch	34

?? Come Misurare La Gravità
or
How To Measure Gravity ¿¿

How To Enter The Fifth Dimension	36
How To Get A Ticket For The Guided Tour	37
How To Celebrate Easter	38
How To Write A First Person Bio One Hundred Words Or Less	39
How To Converse With A Stranger	40-41
How To Write A Third Person Bio Fifty Words Or Less	42
How To Train A Cat	43
How To Win A War Versus Outer Space	44-45
How To Know You've Made It	46
How To Survive	47
How To Go Home Again	48
How To Explain The Birds That Sing At Three In The Morning	49-50
How To Order Off The Menu	51
How To Measure Gravity	52
How To Make The Best Of A Bad Situation	53-55
How To Find The Exact Dimensions	56
How To Make Your Mark	57
How To Prepare For The End	58
How To Make The Elixir	59
How To Find The Way	60-63

??? So finden Sie die Evakuierungsroute
or
How To Find The Evacuation Route ¿¿¿

How To Find God	66
How To Ask Questions	67-68
How To Protect Your Investments	69-70

How To Play Croquet In The Tall Grass   71-72
How To Find The Evacuation Route   73
How To Tell The Time   74
How To Get to the Covered Bridge   75-76
How To Axe Questions   77
How To Write A Poem   78
How To Declare Independence   79
How To Define Remorse   80-81
How To Be Loved   Respected   Famous   82-83
How To Compose The Title Track   84-85
How To Push The Envelope   86-87
How To Tune In To The Bat Channel   88-89
How To Complete Your Collection   90
How To Locate Your Soulmate   91
How To Keep A Secret You Don't Know   92-93
How To Sail Into The Wind   94
How To Pick A Lock   95-96
How To Become One With Nature   97
How To Get Their Blessing   98-99
How To Spot A Cheater   100-101
How To Become The Harbormaster   102
How To Celebrate An Odd Numbered Birthday
   The Day Before Winter Solstice   103-105

How To Give Credit Where It's Due   107

About the Author   109

Incapable of knowing how to ask   I ask
And though the objects of my asking are phantasms
everlastingly   I crave them

Geoffrey Nutter

Passioned pastel neon lights
Light up the jeweled traveler
Who   lost in scenes of smoke filled dreams
Find questions   but no answers

Michael Nesmith

How to Make Questions

Listen to what the spigot
trickle whispers
when toothbrush
rinsing   gristle
   sinew of
half
chewed   undigested
gerunds caught
in molars
   frisk your
self for fake IDs   forgeries
stashed up canals   tiny
cavities   shivved in
fissures   under folds
of hubris flab
   row
to the birchuary   where silver limbs bow over
webbed cliff crags   rim
a shade waved covelet and
capsize
   pound a Known
back to shapeless
dough mound   knead till
your need finally knows
you   then
coil
into
a tasty hook

¿ Comment Faire La Lumière
or
How To Make The Light Come ?

I wish I had me a heaven of my own
Son House

How To Change Your Mind

If it's been over twenty years since you last tried

a braid of black licorice you may now love it
If you come across a bus stop in mid December
    someone may have written *i heart you* with
her finger in the glass's condensation

It may be fresh enough you can tell

where she pressed her forefinger down
hardest and whether or not she wore gloves

It may be that what you think is love

is no more so than a clump of pink insulation
hanging strangely in a trashed storefront

is a freshly butchered ham

If you sleep like a manger scene
boxed in the attic for half a century
    you may be in love   have some rare
form of bipolar   or both   plus   really thirsty

There is an explanation for the river's
freezing only at the mouth of its estuary

    translucent necklace of ice

It may be you will like black licorice
even less than you did twenty years ago
It may be you are actually as alone as you feel
    that it will only exponentiate

or   How To Make Questions

That this is what hides outside in the dark
Listen to me   saying what I know about it

How To Deliver A Toast

To you   October
   what you do to leaves
leaves me
listening for explosions
   tints my butterflies Merlot
   feels me up
without my consent
   puffs me full
of auspicions

And to those who live
with those they share
meals   genes   and germs with
in houses on streets
named for leafy trees

More specifically   to the very old man
at a lake's edge trying to reach
the stick his golden refused to retrieve
To whatever makes him risk falling in
to reach it   The reason
this particular whatever stick matters more
to him than it does to the dog
   who now waits   bored   in the pickup

Especially to whatever causes
the old man to pause   forgetting
the stick   as if listening
   to the calm waves?   drone
of distant traffic?   assuming
hearing aids can find that frequency
   maybe gauging how much
is left before all sound ceases

or   How To Make Questions

And most of all   to you
   lone shiverer   passing lit windows
of strangers on Linden Street
   rubbing cold   bloodfilled hands
and ghosting your breath

How To Hover Above Yourself

If you give the monkey a pet kitten   well
    there are very few
things cuter than a monkey
caring for its kitten
If you give the monkey makeup
and a subscription to *Vogue*
that is fucked up
To give the monkey wings
or desire for wings
is to tumesce it
with your own hard on
for transcendence
To do previously done things
is derivative   unless maybe
done so much better than ever before
The winged monkeys in *Oz*
scared the shits out of me   grinning
abominations   spastic demon droogs
A winged monkey
would do unspeakables
if given a kitten   you wouldn't
even have to show it on
screen   just a close up of its sly
primate face
    hovering over
the furry sleep purring pussy

or   How To Make Questions

How To Protect Your Home

> *There had not been this many words sounded in our house for a long time*
> *and it was going to take a while to clean them out*   Shirley Jackson

It's no longer enough to nail
Father's gold watch chain to a tree
To bury coins and blue marbles in the creek bed
Baby teeth planted only dragons know where

No   Words must now change daily   No Repeats
Must never be spoken aloud
Yesterday's were Turquoise   Deciduous   Portmanteaux

And additional barriers must be built
Monitored   reinforced
Crucifying a thick leather book is a beginning

But you must also curate a new kind of kindling
To scatter it on the intruder's linens   feed his embers
Be prepared to smash the biggest mirror in the house

Splinter the familiar faces trapped inside
Because to truly protect your castle
You must be willing to risk gutting it   roof razed

Attic   a sodden museum
All forty four of Uncle's chapters   published as ashes
Windows stoned   Dresden figurines shattered

Mother's harp toppled
Yes   in the end
You may be forced to let *all* the intruders in
To riot on your turrets and battlements

¿Cómo Hacer Preguntas?

Let them think they broke your golden harp and won
You may have to sleep some nights beside the stream
Slink shadows with black paws   pink pads

But as long as you have
Constance you can reclaim your castle
Inventory your preserves   conjure better barricades
Repair your magic till it's full again

In time the cruelest intruders
Will become your humblest patrons
If they leave words on the stoop?
Burn them in your stove for warmth
If they offer eggs and frosted cakes?
Let them supplement the pumpkin pies and mushrooms
You're learning to grow on the moon

How To Give It A Name

Half a dozen Big Y shopping carts ditched
behind the motel dumpster
   done with rolling   a kind
of wire henge
   conveying only dead
leaves and their own bony shadows

They deserve a collective
noun   a coven
   coagulation   collusion?

And a term for
forsaken corners they congregate
to raise rusty beaks
   squawk a warning
   or issue hissing *plups* of seduction
like a battery
of black crowned night heron bachelors

How To Paint A Still Life

A public hearing will be held on October 30th
on the removal of this tree
The grass is brown beneath the bench

The birches are done   the maple's halfway
Rain's simple project has been all day
The driveway hosts rivulets of weeds

The pictures list at their corners
There are pine needles   sugar maple rotors
in the hallway   asleep on the floorboards

Upstairs is for evening   for pulling shades
A neighbor can be a silhouette behind theirs
    a wave while backing out

A red pick sleeps in the sound hole
    beneath cracked truss rod's shaft
The ice cube trays have grown beards

Ice cube dropped on a desk puddles
out into a wider understanding
of its potential   spawns tributaries

The condemned tree stands silhouetted
by afternoon's neighbor   Tools hang from hooks
    but if they wait   it's not for this

or   How To Make Questions

How To Watch A Summer Sunset

How patient night seems
   even a bit reluctant
How a radiant ruby implodes
   streaks cloudlets peach
   plum   blood orange
How day sinks deeper
and deeper in debt
How time is a kind of mold
How the plane   too high
   clouds too thick to see
How to loons on the lake
   rowing man and boat
might be big noisy ghosts
   solids with power
to produce waves
   interrupt reflections
How the loons vanish   no
   apparate over there
How perfectly their tremolo

How To Play Spin The Bottle

First   a list of all the lips that have touched your own
    a separate one for mermaids
Tiny water bugs seem kissing incessantly
    emanata of radiating ripples   unlike the first
shy nape kiss the baron bestowed upon the baroness
Princess whose SWAK turns
handsome princes into gorgeous gardeners
Pilgrims' chaste kissing of obelisks
their prophets most likely pissed on
There are as many kissings as ways of listening
    the slurpy sound's most ridiculous
They smooched that way in the movie
you said was better than the book
    in the trailer I liked
better than the movie
    tongues twined as if trying
to pull long words out of each other
    digging for grains of paradise
Strange civilizations teem inside us all
    grumbling   sloshing   How many gallons you
have drunk   how many gallons of you *are* you
    how much your lovers' sweet sweat and saliva
End with a list of everything
you haven't been blessed with
occasion to touch lips to yet

or   How To Make Questions

How To Sing And Why

Have you ever stared into evening till foglight fades
    way past the whatever point
you even remember what you started out looking at?

Who hasn't sought a river?
Stood on the bank and thought about it
And wondered about the others

Hear them   those dusky birds piping their beaks off
    mud nests spitglued on a cliff face   their refuge?
Some songs sung simply   sans semitones

    to measure the distance betweens
Some songs are   *it's time to go again*
into the desert resplendent   to lie in the shade of a tall tree

    to reply   *tall trees are good*
good to include in your song

How To Measure The Dew Point

    and how determine
which way it is pointing
    detect what it wants
me to do

    establish
approximate rate
at which I
evaporate

into some matter
of done that lies

just beyond
dew?

or   How To Make Questions

How To Define Perpetual

She stands the point yard
ends
   field begins   alcove
mowed in a tall grass wall

Supplicant digits splayed

as though the preciousness
she's just dropped
has fallen too low for hands

Pupil less   downcast eyes

lost in the same sorrow El Greco
saw there   and won't look

up for the aroma of seared flesh
transmogrifying on the grill
   or the constant roar of a beast

that spits blades at her

Sun   snow   rain
   sleet's slowest striptease
of all but these
last stray
flecks
of paled glaucous
from her robe

   whispering *soon   virgin mother*
   eternity starts so very soon

How to Get Their Attention

Afraid people aren't listening?
You may need to reroute the signal chain
    a louder PA   a crown
made of condenser microphones
    more potent talking points
Describe the rows of miraculous
slag sculptures you're smelting on Primrose Hill
    index tap a bevel square
to inject a subliminal beat
Soon they'll be staring at your macoma
    my word for the point where jawbones meet
    not to be mistaken for sarcoma
    a malignant tumor in connective tissue
They may   in fact   stare at you
like a human person who's sawed off
their own head   then sewn it back on
Comfort them
    No need to be frightened   when stars flatline
    it just means we're traveling at light speed
is a nice lightsaber swoosh segue to
    the most benevolent weapon
    instantly cauterizing each wound it births
    each digit it subtracts
Most important   sustain a steady gush
of wordage   syllabicize till your crown
topples   windscreens and sibilance filters
shatter   till each
organelle smolders
    throat too ash thick
for any sound
but your most utterly sincere choking

or   How To Make Questions

How To Describe Iridescence

The unreachable itch is one way
to say it   A sonic
composed of three or four robins

    slurred phrase of solitary veery
    gray plumbeous back   large white wingbars
    two more   too intermittent to tell who

And to lie for any thing to crawl across
in the first long lawn of late April's
tiny purple and whites   coarse crabgrass
tufts   whole forests of two inch maples

Vapor trails are afterlife
of mica shards
our Huffys kicked up with the dirt
   unmoored pigeon glitter

White throated sparrows nesting
in the rhody hedge again
Watch scrawny hatchlings gullet worms
from the living room window

Stand here when brain's old sneakers
denting the washer   kicking it wide
   or ripped   snagged
flapping in branches plastic bag

Can you make out the mist of pollen
grains shaken free from each anther?
How about now?
Look up like a nestling waiting
for her segment of worm

¿Cómo Hacer Preguntas?

How To Find A Missing Cat

Soggy   pathetic   nearly
unreadable
scrap tacked to a pole
Streaky   smeary
thanks to three weeks' pissy rain
    but stop a few   you can still
make out pink nose
    bushy ruff   long
    stiff briskers
Dead leaves and feathers
askew in her tuxedo
    ruff and pantaloons
seedy from a driveway
dirt bath
Freckled wide verdant eyes
    inquisitive?
    wary
of the lens
    turtle chin
lifted in protest
?

Note use of capped italics in
my eroding shrine   *PLEASE CALL*
    but didn't add
She telepaths thru thrums   vibrations
    dowsing paw pressed o'er your heart
Still enough
intact words   numbers left
    a bundledup stranger   some
next street over
neighbor you'd otherwise
never meet   may risk a
    knock   despite needing both

| or   How To Make Questions

hands to restrain
an ungrateful beast that liked stranger
kibble better
    yowls at being found

How To Make The Light Come

Look at me   I'm introducing myself to the slush mound
the plow left at the foot of our driveway

Here I am   extricating matted clumps from a cat's ruff
as National Public Radio plays me a scherzo by Debussy

I stand before an open window to summon sunrise
    to prove I am naked   to arouse vistas

I'm the winch that lifts up dawn
I'm making the light come

so hard
    she's riding me bareback   like we share a shadow

or   How To Make Questions

How To Make Friends

While light held
I watched for air mass boundaries
   sunspots   troopers snugged behind
median bushes
Tried breathing calmly through
my spiracles   inventoried car models
   diagnosed vanity plates
   attempted rerouting despair   felt
reassured entering *End*
of Reduced Salt Area

   startled by sudden
gasps that punctuate the sleepscape
of the woman next to me   abrupt air shifts
   winds that blow through the pillow
and cradle topography of New England
churchyards   mossy aisles where
her ancestors are interred
   hemmed by pin and feathered stonewalls

If people become friends they may give you
pictures of yourself that they took
   show you how to highlight text
and drag it   rip off bandaids for you
   they may dong you on the head
accidentally with a bocce ball
   let you nap while they drive the first
four hundred miles

   teach you each of the quarter winds
Like poor Uncle Harold   how proud he was
of his first forty foot extension ladder
It must've been Harry who said

¿Cómo Hacer Preguntas?

*somewhere in the middle crease you'll be
riding against 32 winds at once   zag
zigging like crazy and about to blow away
   that's when a fella needs a friend*

or   How To Make Questions

How To Transform Base Matter Into Gold

The officer asks you a question
    and there's just something
in the way he says the phrase
    back there

This officer is likely a kind   gentle man
He wears a bright gold badge
    sidearms snapped snug
in their holsters
But even good people have bad days
    may have a soundproofed
cell in their basement   a vintage
handcuff and scalpel collection

World so gilt and shiny
    determined to abort attention's span
in a mustard bath of distractions
The answer's usually floating in plain sight
    but can only tread water for so long
before drowning in its question

People with words   all CAPS
    stitched into the assseams of their sweats

    EAGLE   PINK   LOVE

The Baptist steeple's paint is cracked   peeling
    crooked

Sorry officer   I didn't see the sign
may not be enough

Look into the sky
like a GPS acquiring satellites

¿Cómo Hacer Preguntas?

How many Canadian geese
in the fraying chevron flying over?

Twenty?
   twenty one
with
the

straggler?

or   How To Make Questions

How To Observe Daylight Savings Time

Shivering has
   softened my pith
to slush
compacted
by combat treads
   snowshoes mostly for
making a path
to the composter
   where I check to see
if winter's first fake
concession speech
has returned
to rank mulch yet
   regurgitated Moo
Goo Gai Pan

Someone lost control
   spun out
right where 220
takes a hard right
   where Unity first touches
its frozen pond
Someone left
a coaster on top
of their half finished pint
and never came back
Pouring me another
   Sally says
we named our best
brown ale after Phil
   but dude never drinks it

How To Pass The Time

Knock his picture off the wall
   tumble down the staircase
This will wake great
great grand's
family daguerreotype

Now stir the iodine   swirl
of mercury vapors
   enter the copper as
it's engraved by bromide of silver

Immerse in the hissing eyes
of solemn   emulsified children
   till you congeal into
their rigid pose   held waiting
for the wizard to emerge
from his velvet hood
   without wiggling   blinking
   sneezing   breathing   and go
on holding a
century and counting

Then blaze back further
   till you reach it
   the last fluid   human instant
before this plate cut
forever stole it   through
the slit aperture
of Sven's smirking eyeroll
   Elsa's yawning uvular invite
to her inraveled whatness

or   How To Make Questions

How To Write A Cover Letter

My old paper route   Gazette
   Ledger   Bulletin   Post   or Times?
What days of week were mine?
Whether news was war   engagements
   obits   or just stacks of glossy
coupons   readymade
to devolve into soaked wads on the stoop?
Weather warm
   wet   cold   noncommittal?
Which bike rolled the named streets of my town
   or did I tread boulevards
   try skipping over the back
breaking cracks?
Who'd trust a kid like that with The News?
   sticky digits   untied kicks   crooked
canines   asymmetrical
sockets   already in training for *this*
   another full grown dullness busy
forgetting every verified event
   each chronicled occurrence?
What shapes of clouds passed over then?
   or were those old timey clouds
designed solely
to staunch sunset's contusions?
   yet pretty sure each time
sheaf I tossed on your stoop
had been rounded   bound before
reaching my hands   affixed
by skinny red rubber bands
   constricting fact checked   above
the fold actualities   stocked
with factual phrases   boilerplated
proofread truths pressed into
existence prior to this
recurving blip's *now*

How To Reach Enlightenment

The man with the metal detector has found
the expression of a pianist's page turner

Except hours   and he's yet to turn a page
He slaloms   saccades in

and out of our personal spaces
     paces beaches   meadows   woods   any

where something may've been left
for him   Reverse coulter

harvesting seeds planted
by chance   steering

with ears   till static fields
bloom into sudden   golden music

How To Complete Your Apprenticeship

Tired of scraping and scrubbing his toxic crust
    the scabbed and peeling lead paint off
his plaster stations of the cross statuettes
    breathing in His wounds' dank decay?

Are you ready to take the Master's brush
    be the one conjuring divinity
      and slaying it
To lash each eye

Constellate each halo
Slash each whip welt
Shine the cruel hammer and nails
Refresh thirsty palm holes

Twist sneers on the mob of spitting thugs
Provide shade for yon herd of timid onlookers
Brush splinters on your own rugged cross
Stroke the thorns on your own bloody crown?

How To Light A Torch

Part of the funeral home's package deal
   why leave it to wither beside his stone?

The center stalk stole what light
a basement window allows
   drank shower's mist   grew to tall   red edged sheath

Perimeter stalks shrank to brittle brown
Pick them away   sit it in stronger light

After Thanksgiving   leave the wishbone beside his name
and dates   then follow   at respectful distance
   sparks from a dragging tailpipe all along Route 2

¿¿ Come Misurare La Gravità
or
How To Measure Gravity ¿¿

Like spines of air   frozen in an ice cube
Weldon Kees

How To Enter The Fifth Dimension

You have one trainee angel who reminds you to send out birthday cards   but voice is faint   half muted by cell towers and cicadas   Best guess?   last sent a birthday card when I was nine

An apprentice angel to remind you not to use sledgehammers or chainsaws when tired   drunk   depressed   but only registers as a dead leaf skittering in hectic wind   may in fact distract   cause crushed or severed phalanges

You have an attention deficit demon who just makes you daydream second period math away   Mostly maroons you with Sylvia in the blue lagoon

Another herds all the angriest rain clouds above you   biggest cliché there is

Can you sometimes nearly hear the atonal unmelodies they hum? Make you sad your petty demons die bored   jealous   sexless   unloved   no angel intern assigned to care   none tiny enough to hold   caress   and *there there* them when they cry?

or   ¿Cómo Hacer Preguntas?

How To Get A Ticket For The Guided Tour

Here   a stalactite has dripped for five thousand years
raising   drip by drip   offspring in the form of this
stalagmite   These tapering incrustations will become
one unified column   geologists predict   in only two
hundred more years

This tree is scion of an ancient elm   beneath its canopy
colonial elections were held   where a Tory tax
collector was tarred and feathered

In this pond   I recently found the flashlight I lost on a
sixth grade Cub Scout trip sixty-five years ago
Coming back from the outhouse at two   its ghostly
beacon drew me to water's edge   No   not offended if
you don't believe me   I simply present the most
reliable version of certain facts as I have come to
understand them

Lastly   this monument atop a lone hill by the old state
mental hospital honoring two *Executed in 1806* and
Exonerated in 1984   for what and why   I don't know
but it's always neatly mown round the stone   and
someone still leaves bouquets   On balmy nights like
this I go with my flashlight and wait

How To Celebrate Easter

Have you ever seen so many ominous cloud formations
so much road-kill on Route 9? Tomorrow   an estranged
possum family will reunite over his pale corpse
maybe catch a comforting glimpse of resurrection
through nimbus gaps   Virginia Slims Smokers of
Whately   why not contribute your butt to the
philanthropist's fountain   already flush with similar
tithes?   Space Prophet Dogon vibrates my dash
rewound twice   No periscopes spotted in the
Connecticut   no snipers visible in the Unitarian
steeples   Some don't care what stamps they get at the
post office   some hold workers hostage for giving a
book of hearts   Good day for deciding to love everyone
or at least nodding your neighbor in passing   leaving a
bouquet on the curb   gravestone of the street
Caution   Solar Glare   Beware   Gibbous Moonlight
Over Winchendon

or   ¿Cómo Hacer Preguntas?

How To Write A First Person Bio   One Hundred Words Or Less

Welcome to my super condensed self blurblet   an ever expanding excitement energy bubble   How many things am I interesting about?   ways you might wish to consider being impressed by? Well   since last withdrawl from my bio bank   see all this interest and dividend accrual? Yet it's awkward   sooo *awk ward*   to jizz a flatter ring of adjectivals over each unique accomplishment   to blow trumpet smoke up my windsock prototype   though I could   with a quick swivel   unscroll my unabridged lists for perusal   for now   allow me to ninjastar this into your temporal lobe   I plucked it from a constellation

How To Converse With A Stranger

for Alvaro de Campos

When I was a kid the Operator was one woman omniscient schoolmarm able to knit while plugging through every call in the world   But now   out the window   every sign's *Corporate Interiors* or *Discount Sleep* marquees warning this movie is *Rated X for Sadness* because even the most divine dreams   the kind I play and rewind for weeks   were manufactured by starving children in a Third World sweatshop

I can't sleep on trains   Past sealed sills the outside world drifts through its own dream   in which I'm required to remain a small but alert part   nativity play shepherd who just has to bow and stare adoringly at the miracle

A dream I do remember   I'm at the door counting my machine's red winks   Instead of messages   though recorded dreams the *apartment* had while I was out   In one I get caught   turn myself in   escape under assumed name   But they keep following and each place needs a new me

Soon unused heteronyms stalk me too   Bowling with colleagues   an almost steady girl   when I'm invaded by Ulrich Flint   Professor Vhümpeltaáz   Juan Doe Luckily   the bathroom window slid open quietly and I only sprained an ankle   Stay a few limps ahead of scorned aliases   quick catch up with your prettiest alibis don't fall in love with anyone or thing you're likely to lose someday

or   ¿Cómo Hacer Preguntas?

Once I step off into my new town   I'll hold out this face like it's mine   Maybe you'll be standing on the platform will gesture for me to come share your umbrella   We could stand quietly together   listen to the rain   and as long as no one speaks   we can postpone our acquaintance   possible engagement   our inevitable parting

How To Write A Third Person Bio   Fifty Words Or Less

Once at a party Daniel put a beer can on his head and tried moonwalking because the girl might laugh   Or the day Danny and his friends were trampolining in Mark's backyard and heard the ice cream song   but by the time everyone ran home and got their allowance money

or   ¿Cómo Hacer Preguntas?

How To Train A Cat

Yes it's true   I'd been pleased   somehow *flattered* by the
mice   as if arrangement of their corpses on the stoop
spelled out   over months   our secret compact in furry
cursive

    but this rain slick corpus of gray   briefly iridescent
feathers   reversed neck   ant clogged eyes   even she'd
seemed to know it was different somehow   to leave
beside

not offer up *on* the slab where I sip my Fog Buster
Didn't I tell you?   *nothing with wings*   I hiss   *Nothing with*
a repertoire of songs   even if most of them are stolen

I'd left the offending rodents displayed a day   *a warning*
but this muted melody of vanes and barbs mocks me   so
I lift with a paper towel strip   repeat my guttural scold

insisting she watch   and making sure no one *else's*
watching   flick it past the lilacs   She lounges
elongates languorously in the driveway   blithely licks
white paws   ruff

haunches   sprawls   sticks a hind leg straight up
antennae like   barely twists to lick clean parts of
herself she shouldn't even be able to reach

How To Win A War Versus Outer Space

?

Derek will play War
    Cowboys & Indians
or Matchbox cars   but
nothing with Outer Space
Outer Space isn't *real*
    he says each time I ask

??

The best was getting shot
on a hill
    the spastic
lurch into
a rapture
of
rolling
and
tumbling

???

One day at recess we played
Nazi and Jew   The jungle gym
was our concentration camp

or   ¿Cómo Hacer Preguntas?

When we couldn't find enough
kids to play Jews we forced
Debbie Weintraub
We *learned* it in Social Studies
   Tim explained to the principal

????

They came back with a bb gun   nunchucks   a
Louisville Slugger   buck knives   a Jart   and a flame
thrower *can of hairspray and a lighter*   The guys on my
side had squirt guns   cap guns   M16s that sound like
popcorn poppers when you pull the plastic triggers   I
misunderstood too   brought my blue lightsaber
batteries almost dead

How To Know You've Made It

Each state erects a billboard to welcome me   No longer just a wasp caught between panes   a daft seminary dropout   It's more in my interest to show how a flood works than stay dead for the rest of my life   If Swiss cheese were named after me I'd be the perfect marriage of dairy and air   Drink straight from a bottle that vows to make my coughs more productive   Sleep upon a chest of drawers   the moon   lemon on the sill relief

How To Survive

Our fifth grade field trip was a sleepover in the Natural History Museum   Mark   Dave   and I chose the Great Rift Valley Room   lay in sleeping bags surrounded by zebras   lions   giraffes   hippos   and cheetahs   Their glass eyes glowed   moved   in the beam of my flashlight   We were a secret tribe of Bedouin wizard warriors   As chief's son   I kept watch while the others slept   An enemy tribe in the nearby Rain Forest Room worshipped a brutal god   were whispering bloody tales   cackling   I tightened grip on the sacred ibex horn dagger of my people   One wizard practiced spells in his sleep   which you could mistake for snoring   another dreamt he's the only ant in Antarctica   But one zebra stayed awake with me all night   shared ancient alchemies only mystic zebras know   a really cool zebra   and I was glad the taxidermist hadn't trimmed her long eyelashes

How To Go Home Again

We're holding hands and excited to show my lake but always end up something else instead   *Cedar Lake must've drained over night*   I explain as we slowly muck an alien swamp named Memory Lake Stripped Butt Naked But For Bottles   Candy Wrappers   Dead Rafts   Wilted Lilypads   Fish   None Big As The Ones They Told Us We Were Fishing For

Somehow it *is* still my lake   but what if now I'm left forever sinking into this ugly unlake of suck beneath it? *Forever* meaning what it always   *Always* meaning same   How time cuts a wake   then keeps itching   itching   the seams of that cut to infection   a pus of memories that leave a scab   a mud crater left after childhood's lake has reseeded the clouds

or   ¿Cómo Hacer Preguntas?

How To Explain The Birds That Sing At Three In The Morning

?

One book will tell their names   parse these notes   this sequence

On another shelf nothing exists

Sentry in distant outpost listens   whispers in his broken transmitter

   clarity of their polyphony

fluid arpeggiousity

   rate of warblato

     trills decay in cirrus seas of skyverb

??

They are conducting market research   broadcasting commercials

Programming would not be possible without the underwriter's support

     Nature's finest organic nesting adhesive

   Worms sweet as hummingbird nectar

How To Make Questions

Chirping bogus stats to clinch an argument

    have found their nest on Google Earth
    are calling me over to see   posting

me pokes   friend requests   Live
Tweeting the night   flirting with air traffic controllers

    mimicking the scene where Sonny
gets shot up in *The Godfather*
    chirping an impossibly fast snare strafe

They've tempo mapped their wingflaps   comparing
BPMs

???

Faintly hover inside my pet flying dream   initiate into
its secret society   clothe insomnia in its silky kimono

????

Fledgling wants to know
    do mouses grow up to be rats?
    do worms ever eat birds?
    Where does sky end?

or ¿Cómo Hacer Preguntas?

How To Order Off The Menu

I'll start you off with a glass of ice water some silly kid
left out overnight on a dare   Next   a place setting
that happens to accentuate your server's tones   that is
mine

Allow me to dim the lights   turn them off
completely   Surely you've dined in the warm cone
provided by a steady   patient   flashlight bearer?
Dining music? How about total

silence? Or perhaps four unsynchronized gamelan
orchestras? True   they may dissonate through hors'
d'oeuvres and entrée   but by dessert   I promise they
shall mellifluate

serene as parallel paths of moonlight on Europa's
frozen sea   a solid surface given depth like this   by
clear vertebrae of air   As it melts   feel free to sip the
icy distillation of my

first distinct memory slow or swift as you like whilst I
present a brief   but generously detailed   recitation of
our locally sourced specials   or are you ready for the
check?

How To Measure Gravity

Is it true that gravity moves a hundred eighty six thousand miles a second? They are eighty percent sure Between sneezes I heard most of what you said Was it how it made you sad that the quasar's light's only bent by Jupiter's gravity once a decade? Was it that you love me? I'll lose 40 pounds in my lifetime shedding dead cells assuming I don't die before a lifetime   assuming there *are* any chicken strips left to be ladled from this tub of tikka masala sauce   enough unbroken spokes to carry me home   See the intaglio of my balding radials in your gravel? They say sun rays take eight minutes to reach us When I dropped my keys it seemed about that   the long weightless waiting for splash   There is no up and down in space   no diagonal   no sepia tones   Earth   less than a pollen speck in infinity   Why must facts be such frowning   homely things   and space   so godawful cold dark   lonely? It's predawn fiftythree miles below the thermosphere   when birdcalls begin ricocheting off of each other   meaning back to gravity   time for mass

or   ¿Cómo Hacer Preguntas?

How To Make The Best Of A Bad Situation

Do you have any menthol lights?

You call that twig pile a gallows?

Are you casting the first stone because you're without sin or because you were first to find a good stone?

Is it too late to go with the guillotine?

How To Make Questions

Could I have crescent eyeholes cut in my blindfold?

Would folks over five feet make sure they aren't obstructing the view of any children or otherwise height disadvantaged persons?

How do I know you won't arrange my corpse in absurd or obscene poses?

Isn't a noose just a halo grown tired of hovering?

or   ¿Cómo Hacer Preguntas?

Rather than repent   may I express remorse via frail rue tinged falsetto of a yodel?

Are you casting the first stone because you were unable to pry loose any bricks?

Do you always light strangers' cigarettes so tenderly?

Do you have any plans for later on this evening?

How To Find The Exact Dimensions

When I sneeze *really* hard I can tell the exact dimensions of my soul   squinting my mind is like trying to see what flakes in a snow globe spell   jogging laps in a shrinking cul de sac   Instead of completing tasks   I freeze in the spine of thoughts

The whole world is always happening everywhere all at once

In each glass of ice water I see ships trying to hit icebergs

Some nights I wonder why my parents never told me my middle name   A man in a lime tuxedo screws an honorary plaque into my forehead when I doze   or rather   he *resumes* doing so   announces   *there will be a buffet   followed by foxtrots on his catafalque*

But tonight I'm getting lubed on dollar drafts at The Vic Monika asks for detailed directions to all my happiest places just for the fun of guessing my accent Then argues with Nora about which pretty movie star I most remind them of

The dimensions   they vary wildly from second to second   sneeze to sneeze   gusty days blowing into a hole in the air that can't be measured yet   that won't fill till it's swallowed all the light

or   ¿Cómo Hacer Preguntas?

How To Make Your Mark

With a brown haired girl I spoke to for less than eighteen seconds   with her floppy labradoodle Beaumont   even with that creepy death's head rat tail possum skullinking in my headlights

How'd I never notice the microchips in dragonfly wings? The way they catch the light? For I   too   have descended from dragons   In my lair there's gold enough to buy a sunny kingdom by the sea   So *fuck* this waiting for clearance from the tower to land   no longer an heir on the side of caution   I'll strut the prickly plank declare   *I am a fact wearing improper pants   come touch my new haircut   let's breakdance on the outside of enough   let's all mosh in the Extension Corridor*

   but I raised the screens   lowered the storms when I got home   Nervously paced the perimeter of my little life   tried looking purposeful in case neighbors were watching   Began writing this   to you? Cut   then pasted back on the page   hit *save as*

How To Prepare For The End

Sky burial on K2 had come highly recommended   to impale my final vampire stem   snip my poltergeist's tenacious frays   best aerial view of my victory lapse reel screened in Digitally Restored Technicolor   vivisect memories one last time with my pallbearers   sweet shy guys from Youth Group   A prominent parishioner was also nice enough to attend my Perishing   to inscribe my slate slab   *Failed Botany Experiment*   *Born in the Heights Passed in freakish hailstorm*

But when I reclined in my sarcophagus   only salt from your ducts touched my lips   only your hands tried to pluck my heart from the flames   I tried too   for me for you my love   and no more summer days on the river to cry   laugh   sing   scream *Help*   though after all my time and money spent on arrangements   after spending all time's money one entertains grave estrangements   and see how still   hands crossed eyeshadowed just so   lids shut sewn

all of a sudden   not just *some* of a sudden   all my parts were not longer just rehearsing our omission

or   ¿Cómo Hacer Preguntas?

How To Make The Elixir

A kill   a crick   a forlorn bleat   a streak of tigers   a creak and swiveling of oars in sockets   a crinkling of to go bags   pop tops   confetti of scimitars   jumper cables   cairns   a cough   a snort   a nostril divesting itself of snot   a retort   done and dusty words   each higher in the fog index   a knack for always choosing other lost tourists when asking directions to a dream you can tell is   and try to steer through its smoke extract cerebral soot   without whiteknuckling the wheel sufflating the dream   to incisor grip the shiniest apple and rise   lashes dripping   from that aether into this pitching present perfect tents   flapping   flailing   flying

How To Find Your Way

Drink and be whole again beyond confusion   Robert Frost

?

Start walking on the asphalt road thru village   Ignore side paths following road going round   Take right till not on roads any more end of village entering forest   Continue trail going up   Path could get difficult because bushes like blackberry   Feel free to pick if season is right   We reach fountain   water drinkable if not dry

??

Path ahead maybe unclear with fallen trees   Trail in swirls right and left   Many dears pass here maybe want to say hi   We reach bushy peak on left and think forest behind on your right   We do *not* take U Turn   Go most left and down not dry bed on left but straight follow ridge decent gradual   After some meters enter forest to swap meadows and forests   Walk head up not to miss when path splits but we are right   Careful not to miss as decent becomes steeper reaching tree passage mark red   Keep swirling path past animal shelter in plum tree orchard   Left is a bench for a rest of your fancy

???

After a while our ways splits   both work to meet again further   Path soon finishes a lonely tree crossing another path   There turn left east southeast directive   Our right we see central ridge of range   As you decent will see a memory plate if not lost in tall grass

or ¿Cómo Hacer Preguntas?

This area may be little confusing   There is no clear path   Simply find a way   Stream is behind   Follow the current leading to old hotel that do not exist any more

????

The path will split five ways we ignore staying straight on   Also ignoring parallel paths at another small meadow and crosspaths all directions   See yellow triangle on tree? Could be covered by branches then another small meadow   Path clearly left but keep small one forward   Make next straight few hundred meters   White red markings are hunting path which we certainly *do not* want to follow   Keep narrow trail entering beech wood   We walk upstream small pretty river may or not be drinkable now

?????

Trail accent left slope of glen and very old forest past small stream and next 15 cross stream again keep on left   Reach a meadow staying right till emerging NW but not diverging if we reach forks depending if locals are using other trails   Keep straights soon to pass area where national hero was executed for organizing rebellion against Ottomans and reach a T junction   Bit further see white green markings? It might be some ropes blocking the way   We walk past them

??????

We reach junction with abandoned bus and detrituses behind fence   Take wide earth path right to follow metal rods guide us a while   Path splits but keep main which led to a U   Turn the right follow horizontal slope reaching for small wooden hut   Way left and climbs

How To Make Questions

steep to ridgetop   soon to divide   Go right coming to view point forward on the one up not left that takes you under the hill   See? We are now the highest peak

???????

After enjoying we continue path to small naked hills   Cross path forward to reach big meadows fruit trees   There is no clear path   Walk down right crossing bushy dried creek   See barbed wire in front? Follow reaching a river   Get the shoes off and cross

????????

Take accenting path and continuing left of monastery   Ignore road right and up follow blue marks on the up to pines   Sometimes white red marks   Slight left narrow single track   See bigger trees green arrow pointing direction on it? Watch for this point may be difficult   Cross orchard exiting right up through   A few hills we can see around but we clump it on the narrow path to small monument on top   Past monument steep grassy slope yet stay on to the middle   Make brakes drinking water for this steep accent

????????

On top a rock with green red mark   We continue path right to meadow full with bracken   Stay right slope on ridge   Path is unclear in a bushy area like tunnel of vegetation steep and surrounded and last part rather rocky   Plastic strings tightened for some branches help our direction   A nice beech forest   Path difficult but faint yellows on trees and blue arrows on some rocks   A meadow emerges walking line between forest and meadow but up   Splendid view to village and surrounding peaks good spot for breath

or ¿Cómo Hacer Preguntas?

?????????

From viewpoint turn back   The peak you saw is our next directive   We need to to get on a path on its foot   After path makes right before peak starts down into forested part   Keeping follow to meadow on a saddle and point of view and usually goats

??????????

At splits we take on the crossing meadow one continues in forest towards right   We reach U turn with a nice little just on the inside   See two houses? Path takes us between near left house with barking dog   At orchards our path becomes invisible   Just cross it   Path may return toward the end to cross small stream with drinkable water turn   From there see the road right to next village? Tomorrow's steps are written and waiting there

??? So finden Sie die Evakuierungsroute
or
How To Find The Evacuation Route ¿¿¿

> The headless man was sitting like a murdered anchorite
> discalced in ashes and sark
>
> Cormac McCarthy

How To Find God

After fire   but before inventing
the wheel
   before humming
and drumming on the wheel
while stuck behind a salt
truck on the highway
   wondering   *if feet have souls*
why don't hands?
Now he's yawning
   counting stained glass bleps
during pastor's Leviticus sermon
   and always late
for first period science
   where they say the horizon
escapes us at fourteen miles

How To Ask Questions

They say *no such thing*
as a dumb one
   but let's acknowledge
all the honorable mentions
   like *how are you doing?*
Let's wear glassed skull displays
   sext each other hi res brain
scan porn   closeups of the folds
   crevices   cracks
cached knots in our
squishy   private mind parts
   x ray uncertain gray matters
only growing less and less
certain   grayer   greyer
finally flooded by addictive
drip of dreams   or   to add
tinsel to injury   drained by
dementia
   cognition puddles
calcifying into polyps
   smug memes misquoting
Jefferson
   so best keep spinning
that axis   swinging
dull axes in
the vast tick infested question
pricker thickets   or morph
right quick   be
come that rando who pocket
dialed you at a work friend's
wedding
   poked through
on just the smallest
half bar of static

¿Cómo Hacer Preguntas?

hiss reception
   and I'm all like *Hello?*
   Hello? Hello?
   Who the hell is this?

or　　How To Make Questions

How To Protect Your Investments

Baseball bat under the bed's

rolled to where I can't

reach

　　Probably nothing　　small

nothing bumping littler nothing

　　except you heard it　　too

So I'm lying naked

on the floor　　breathing

hard　　fleeced to shoulder

in the vast dust preserve

Sound

a short distance

from inaudible　　door flexing

in frame　　quarter turned knob

　　storm pane inching

Sound that plans to rape and kill us

　　steal all of our favorite things

knows our pins

passwords   prompts   secrets

even if there was

no sound

or   How To Make Questions

How To Play Croquet In The Tall Grass

Trees have no choice but lean
where the sun tells them to

There was a gray with its heart
ripped out and a disemboweled chipmunk
face down on the porch like tiny   lumpy rugs
I hate to sound ungrateful
The day turned out a lot nicer
than expected   meaning the weather
Meaning the boss was
out   and I walked into town with Kurt
Only two dogs were forced to wear sweaters

Later I spread the wet books on the sidewalk
    which only left them more warped

By my situation   I mean the place
where I am seated
A swatch claims it's painted
Mirror Lake   green so pale
it almost isn't   One darker
on the swatch spectrum is *Mint Truffle*
    exact shade of reed rimmed bog
by the DMV

I play against myself   each ball turns
poison   then defects into the jewelweeds

I watch a two and three year old
shift between Power Ranger
and a dialect of Transformer
    follow a trail of feathers that fails
to arrive at a corpse

The swifts eat the tiny insects
  a manna their favorite god gave them

How To Find The Evacuation Route

Time to get poked in the third eye
   I say to my sleeping third eye
Show me your perfect fucking silken tapestry
   I demand of the spider spinning inside my sound hole
Think how much lonelier you'd be without the fog
   I remind my suicidal lighthouse keeper

The double hung that only goes halfway down
   our frayed screen
view of yard gods sinking
below the jewel weeds

Rich left a message   *nothing to worry about*
   just the exhaust shield
The guy at Aubochon said   *it's all just fiberglass now*
   it's not even real anymore

Your freckles are really starting to blossom
   I mean that in a pretty way   mean I want to kiss each

You should be flattered   so many mosquitoes intent
on imbibing your salty sweet   on carrying your wine off
past the tree line
   one tiny red sip at a time

How To Tell The Time

    meanwhile   the birds all
sing their certain song
    reprise a string of notes
we know are true

*   it's that time of
day and season   I'm here
    no worm in my beak
how about you   you   you?*

How To Get To The Covered Bridge

When ceiling fan's ticking too
fast   impatient clock
that barely dents this swollen
air   marooning you twenty
thousand leagues over the sea
    know   mortal   only fullest
immersion will suffice
    Follow the centenarian shaking
scraped grit off her scratch ticket
out the driver side window
    its glittery path
of
silvery
filigree
    quasar's spectral
signature through space
so muggy
    hazy humid   so
beaded with the sweat
of all your big sticky expectations
See the kids cracking
wise   huffing August fumes   rolling
coolers on wheels downhill   boom
boxes already dialed
to a humbucking flange
flutter solo? No gray cumuli   no black
copters haunt the power lines
    no car alarms bonking   just
the holy river waving
you on   ropeswing swaying
bridge's underspine
    so stop tensing
    burrowed frau   lift
off from this sweltering tarmac

¿Cómo Hacer Preguntas?

    give yourself to the river   what else
can slice through this
lead welkin   purge
pores polluted wet with longing?
It's too bright for eyes'
comprehension   but
don wayfarers and see?   there
on the other shore?   the summer
you you always knew you could be

or   How To Make Questions

How To Axe Questions

First   unknot   if
possible
   line 'em up on the block
   sharpen your gray till it gleams
   then swing
with every

phantom

wing

you've

got

¿Cómo Hacer Preguntas?

How To Write A Poem

I walk her home and there's nothing
we don't talk about   so well

unrehearsed   afraid we'd never be
this alone again

   replies more complete

than months' unbroken solitude   her
voice trellises   steeps   insinuendoes

   continues my ellipses

leads me into dark woulds   churns
my best questions into interrobangs

   words too   though we
don't speak   so sure no

one had ever deserved
one more

   tho music's a newer
sign language since she passed thru

her door   into reflected faces
   a windowed widow watching her watch we

or   How To Make Questions

How To Declare Independence

I could learn how to worship ferns
    but forget not to bring
my indoor voice
outside   not to
choke on a small piece
of air   so much

slips since my datum
retired to Sky Fi Cloud Resort
    aerial fluff
safe   archiving snaps
    awe full apes

awake to mist   drips
from a branch that glistens
        listen

How To Define Remorse

        ?

Verb   A long black car carrying caskets
The first really warm day
   and radio's more tortured prisoners
   more kids in cages
Scattered snow cays
in rhododendron shade
Homeless busker plays *Turn The Page*
   but I need these quarters for the meter

Suddenly there are nearly naked women
everywhere   discalced   pale but alive
They seem so in love with the sun
   and the sun is
loving them back so hard right now
   as sirens saw the air for
elsewheres   toward someone being attacked
by their own heart
   hit by invisible shrapnel   a
shrill that should
rip through
the husk of us all

or   How To Make Questions

??

The same two kids play
with their tiny white dog
in the parking lot
of the motel where they live
   chase it to the dumpster   try

to make it chase them back
   while the mom lights up again
   squints   seems measuring
with slit eyes how much post
dusk light's left   takes
a long   deep
drag on it

¿Cómo Hacer Preguntas?

How To Be Loved   Respected   Famous

There's nothing I couldn't do for you
You could cast me in an instructional film
    a CPR re certification video
    the doofy guy joshing
with coworkers in the cafeteria
who suddenly collapses   wracked agonal gasps
    and I'd turn it into an epic time
travel mind fuck   the first in a Watch Instant trilogy
    and *everyone* will recognize
the starlet who resuscitates me
For I'll reveal the true *you*   overlooked till now
    but always right there   squirming
in their laser pointed crosshairs   air vibrating
around you   prepared for impact

As bassist in your band
I'll throw down a strong   steady throb like you want
    funk out when the jam demands it   but
no proggy five string shit   and oh   the sweet
    shimmering mirage of my falsetto b vox
I will bring you the coldest beer in the green room
I will re up your freshments

Hitch my wagon to your supernova
    I'll purify by reverse osmosis   give you a total
rebrand   juice up acceptance speeches
    pimp the flashing gifs in your electro press kit
    minimize pushback   pump up
uptick   upskirt the competitions' umbrellas
    make your *you*ness POP
Take the way folks feel
about fragrant screensaver meadows at dusk
    expand that supple feeling past every event horizon
    the way power line paths go on forever

or   How To Make Questions

Over time everyone   *everyone*
will come to associate every single tingle of tenderness
    each thrilling awe shiver with you and your deeds

Do you require a lover
that brings it like a suffragette harem triple decker
armada?
    or more amenable
to a hammocked windchimey situation?
    because I've been known to throw
down an intensely chill windchime listening party for two

¿Cómo Hacer Preguntas?

How To Compose The Title Track

Without slipping off into unconsciousness
    make yourself as comfortable as possible

Be quiet as spores molting
on the thickest unread books
in a flooded apartment
    no   loud as the clumpy clouds
of frog larvae on Etna Pond
    lilypad hosting a dragonfly orgy

For example   when motifs grow softer
than disintegrating puffs of clove smoke
    or vague and erratic
as Sisyphus' pint glass sphere smears
    sing the king mattress stuck
halfway up the stairs

Be willing to admit you beat
up the wrong guy on accident
Pound a crooked nail straight again
    scrape burnt crust of failure off the toast

See how the Lou Reed Jack o' lantern
has aged a decade since Thursday   singed
wrinkles widening   caught tween thought
and expression? He's eavesdropping
on your ghost

Make yourself as
uncomfortable as possible

Do you find you can't stop smelling the sweat
between watchband and skin?
Do you tap your toes to the AM Gold piped in front

or   How To Make Questions

    or fuzz crunk dishwashers crank out back?
When you hear children screaming in the distance
    do you choose to believe they're screams of glee?
Remember when Maria told Franz to have a crush
on the questions themselves?
There are more than 12 sextillion stars in this universe
From here they look like God's full arsenal aimed at you

¿Cómo Hacer Preguntas?

How To Push The Envelope

If you've read his palm you know
how many times a man can cut himself
trying to seal an envelope
on that hour when shadows have nails
    is this why he sealed
it with séance candle wax?

The paper he wrote on   hardly above suspicion
    another failed attempt at being the window
name and coordinates show through

The phrase translated into six languages?
Same trick the phone company pulls
    pretending to be thorough

The ink   at least   is to be believed
    especially in such confident cursive?

A man can do many things and go many places
    but   detained by snagged parachute
must contrive means to unsnag

Reasons may seem obscure   still   may appear
after finding his wrist   inexplicably   forty
minutes fast   for
Man can spend approximately
four millennia waiting
at the drafty table near the door
    the very American
Heritage illustration for *anticipatory*
    one last mountain blocking his Beulah view
    yet a minute before she   at last
arrives   an entire sixty seconds remain to shred

| or   How To Make Questions

each word he's fastidiously groomed   entombed
   reperforate each smoothed out façade

¿Cómo Hacer Preguntas?

How To Tune In To The Bat Channel

He watched the cave door
slide back into the cliffside
Flipped off the high beams

    but left the key in   just sat there
    listening to his mask's breathy rasping

Too damn tired   beat up
to lift ass off seat   go inside
    floss   take out his lenses?

Cape bunched and twisted
like a dog's gnawed chew toy

    rear view mirrors a profile
    his dripping   sad   melting wax
museum reproduction

    begins fiddling the dial
    finds some
blowhard pundit's snark

    cloaked in crackly right
wing static
    lowest denom
satellite squawk

then   is snatched   ripped
    to microscopic
jags of hiss

Sighs   starts
to rise   sinks back   scribbles

or   How To Make Questions

on a sticky
replace timing solenoid sensor
fix front end alignment

¿Cómo Hacer Preguntas?

How To Complete Your Collection

I watched my first monarch
drown on diminishing air
beneath a glass
   watched its flutter
slow to brief   shallow
twinge   My first swallow
tail emerged
from the chrysalis
of crimson
wrapped cigar box

Sight keeps spilling
in   filling me up with
colors   especially the dark
hours   when they escape shadow
boxes to shiver
my crown   cocoon my
head in an extended curriculum
of tuning to timbres
no longer
near   prolonging the last
whiff of fading   trusting
incandescence only at the outer edge
of gloaming

Today?   another sublime July
specimen in my close   humid
study   setting down forceps
   readjusting
the light   pinning my wingtips
in a labelled box
   glass held steady   as though it
wasn't already empty
   filled with everything there is

or   How To Make Questions

How To Locate Your Soulmate

I sought your true
name beneath the paw
pads of
your panther
   in your
coelacanth's breath
   spittle
of the song

bird nesting
the roots
of your mountain
range
   checked next

to your register   by
the pillow mints
   shivered awhile in
your walk in cooler
   quested way
back there   where
the p in
cupboard is kept

   was it back
washed
in your glass
of mead?
I swallow
it? It
swallow
me?

How To Keep A Secret You Don't Know

About how it feels when I finally find her
   my imaginary friend   a homeless hand
drummer in Grand Central   flatting palms
on a djembe   tapping ducttaped
boots on tambourines   straw hat brims
with sweaty   crumpled bills
Eyes shut so long I wonder
   has she gone blind?
Try talking shanty treeforts   wonky
catapults   skating the oxbow
   God's mossy
sideburns wilding the altostratus   but
she just nods   Cheshire grins
   eyes shut tighter   drumming
   humming   keening in
a scratchy tongue
   lets me guess what she
recalls   *feels* like recalling
   but if I come here every day
she may finally teach
me how to play
   or sensei flowing   to disarm
assailants by dance
so slow   hypnotized by
the whites of reflected eyes
   say dreams don't
have to come true
to make us happy
   she'll hand me the wing
I supposed blown off my cardinal
whirligig   flown away
to Foreverlandia
   give back grampy's
army knife I thought long

or   How To Make Questions

dropped and rusting Carol Stream
   a show and tell of
lost boy treasures   sequined
piñata fodder she
stole
   explain why nothing
becomes really
real till it's
really gone

How To Sail Into The Wind

Last roll before life went fully digital
    some bright popcorn day   early oughts
sailing with Joel and Ray in Sebasticook
    cutting a wide   frothy wake   few
knots less than a Nantucket
sleigh ride   cigars   chips   Rolling
Rock tallboys   Clouds   crumpled
to dos against the blue   Lazy
smiles   sunblind squints below the boom
    dancing emanata of sun glint lake
Cap'n Ray's released tiller   dangles
bony legs over the gunnel   shouts a toast
    we're far enough out now
    who knows which way our mooring lies?

or How To Make Questions

How To Pick A Lock

?

Ever found yourself
trying to unlock your house
with your car key
    see if it can be started up
    driven
to the weedy   vacant lot
you were meant to fill
    keep leaving more
and more vacant?

??

Ever look at your chain
    find you're still
lugging silver   gold dangling
keys to
nothings
    totaled Toyota   ex's
apartment
    Kryptonite left rusting
on a sign post in the nineties?

???

I swear once the wrong
key
tricked the lock
    seduced its

¿Cómo Hacer Preguntas?

grooves   *Click*
   and the
impossible swung
wide
   fun to remember
when doing
that fumbly
   unconsummated dance
   when right key's all
friction   no fire
   nubbed notches   tired
from twisting
   too lock smoothed to
bring its key
hole to unhinged
orgasm any more

????

Ever notice how brightly
keys shine after five
cycles in the washer
   as though psyched
to admit
you   like *nothing's*
locked so tight
we can't get in with
a bit of lucky jiggling
   nothing so in
coherent the right key
can't be in
serted   *Click*
   turn it
outcoherent?

or   How To Make Questions

How To Become One With Nature

Small birds
don't live
very long

Mayflies much shorter

A creek may lie
fallow fifty years
   to wake one sated spring
    rage wilder
    wider than before

Sequoias seem forever till they aren't

Death dies different out here
Blue dollar hawk's perimeter sweep
yields a house finch
   no house   no heaven   no tears

The resurrected creek
makes crinkly sounds
   a kid feeling
her Christmas present
under the dying spruce
   trying to guess

     before ripping it open

¿Cómo Hacer Preguntas?

How To Get Their Blessing

You can't get them the way you used to
No more rams wait calm in the thicket
for their meek throats to be slit
No old blind Bible dude'll be tricked
into handing over bro's birthright
by doofy strips of trim on your wrists
No more flaming chariots   whirlwind ascensions
In 21C a bodacious sneeze's the quickest way
In one tribe   sneezer preemptively proclaims
   I am now blessed
So don't waste another sacred sneeze
on the void   smother gifts in corporate tissues
   which is why I always greet you
with my most robust noseburst
as you enter my airspace
Till then   gaze into direct sunlight
   sing from musty hymnals   snuff peppercorns
   pollinated dustbunnies   absorb a brass slide's
shimmy through notched resonator cones
Another tribe claims blast radius
correlates to bounty of blessing
   Achoos spraying rafters
shorten the length of your curse
   say ancestors sleep
in saliva   that we only need
spit in a tube to
wake them   retrace their route
   why not snot   too?
They say operators
are standing by   but we know most
are seated   have likely never
performed a risky operation
They say your heart
stops

or   How To Make Questions

for a second
each time   true   but a brusque
   three hundred mile per hour sneeze
also expands soul circumference
   boldly announces an increase in fortune

How To Spot A Cheater

Far
finally
caught up

with near
   text fuzzled
   too minute

for foci
   fine
print no longer

findable
   squinting
only

goes
so
far
   and smeary

head
light
haloes
across

Coffin
Memorial Bridge
at night

   no choice
but cheat

or   How To Make Questions

if I hope
to peep

more
curvy
seraphs

How To Become The Harbormaster

for Ursula K. Le Guin and REM

Digesting shipping routes   tides
    signal chain of underground cables
is fine for an apprentice

    but master must knit her harborcoat
of cove breeze and cormorant feathers
    lace harborboots with strips of kelp

stride white caps
during March's coldest snap
    connect isthmus without sinking

    find fluency in sibilance
of seals   crustaceans
    must deliquesce a mollusk's mantle

till valves part to uncraw
the crosshatched schematics
    earn you your harborname

How To Celebrate An Odd Numbered Birthday The Day Before Winter Solstice

One day gets so much credit
and blame   though took
nearly four hundred in

haling   exhaling   con
suming   jaywalking
   sleepwalking
   so much sleeping or trying to

   and trying and trying to sleep
with other people
   a muchness of rushing

toward flowy abstractions   wisped a
long by spurts of impatience
   my mom once jumped a

cross a parting draw
bridge
in Chicago   didn't

feel like
waiting
   left her friend

on the other side
   unsure if she'd died

   now stoops
over walker   inches
through brain bracken
   chats with the dead

¿Cómo Hacer Preguntas?

    forgotten
every name
but Jesus
    impatient with this
living   impatient just
to see Him

The cat implies I'm to blame
after whining to be let out
Sleet falling on snow crust

    sounds raining needles
I blame leafless trees
for jagged sunset's unfriendly fire
    blame premature sunset for
fourteen hours of cold dark

    moldy fur on the sourdough starter
    nostalgia for the dank
basement hangs of the nineties

I'm an odd
numbered man who explains
to a cat that winter's not his fault
    who tries explaining winter
to the solstice

by scribbling
on receipts I stuff
in emergency brake's hollow
    to forget till it's time
to buy a new preowned ride

or   How To Make Questions

    leaf beneath another list
of impossible Resolutions

    Create a diversion
    then my spies sneak
in and take over the building

    but flesh is weak
    slurps sweets
    rusts resolve

How about one   become
a more lucid listener   sure
    I hear the whetted scythe
of the buzzard's cry overhead
    I want to rootdrop

on tree gossip
    on extinct species
petitioning for reinstatement
    hear what distaff
says to skein

Fat clouds yanked to skinny wisps
    gripped by this
    this   and
this
almost
shortest
day's
drift

How To Give Credit Where It's Due

Thanks to the editors of the following journals and websites who published earlier versions of several of these poems   *Bateau   A Far Cry   Goodfoot   Ixnay   The Ixnay Reader   Left Facing Bird   Leveler   Meat For Tea   The NonBinary Review   nth position   Paragraph   Stirring   Storm Cellar   Route Nine   Qarrtsiluni   Right Hand Pointing   Quarter After Eight   Slant   Verse Daily*

How To Deliver A Toast appeared in the *Poet's Seat Silver Anniversary Anthology*

Extra special thanks my Po posse for helping me make better questions over the years   especially Corwin Ericson   Chris Janke   Kristin Bock   Janel Nockelby   Karen Skolfield   Grinny   and Mahoney   to Alison for translation assistance   Dara   Dobby   and Bill for having my back   Chatula Tova for spiritual guidance   James Lowe for being my funk soul brother   and especially to Shira   for asking all the best questions

This book is dedicated to Frances June Hales

About the Author

Daniel Hales is the author of the hybrid novel, *Run Story* (Shape&Nature Press), and three poetry chapbooks: *Shake My Ashes* (Beard of Bees), *Blind Drive* (White Knuckle), and *Tempo Maps* (Ixnay), which comes with the companion CD *Miner Street Symphony*. His poetry, flash fiction, and hybrid writing have appeared in *Verse Daily*, *Conduit*, *Booth*, *Quarter After Eight*, and many other journals. He rocks out with The Frost Heaves and Hales, The Ambiguities, and Umbral. Umbral's second album, *F#requency 14*, is forthcoming from Spork Press. He lives on a minor street in western Massachusetts but is happiest in his kayak.

More from Frayed Edge Press

More Poetry!

The Ghettobirds by Bryant O'Hara
The Splooge Factory by Christina Springer

More Fiction!

The Flying African by Areg Azatyan; translated by Nazareth Seferian
Blessed Hands: Stories by Frume Halpern; translated by Yermiyahu Ahron Taub
Loose in the Bright Fantastic by E.B. Moore
Songs for the Gusle by Prosper Mérimée; translated by Laura Nagle
Street Smart X 7 : A Street Smart Series Omnibus edited by Alison M. Lewis
DIG by Robert Paul Moreira
In Madison's Cave: A Novel by Douglas Anderson
Ambushing the Void sby James McAdams
Bellapalma by Jens Bjørneboe; translated by Esther Greenleaf Mürer
Ere the Cock Crows by Jens Bjørneboe; translated and with a reconstruction of the play by Esther Greenleaf Mürer
Right Guy, Wrong Time by Louise MacGregor
Stealing: A Novel in Dreams by Shelly Brivic

More History and Politics!

"Do Not Misunderstand Me": The Collected Radical Addresses to the Unity Congregation (1888-1891) by Hugh Owen Pentecost, edited by Robert P. Helms
Jeremiah Hacker: Journalist, Anarchist, Abolitionist by Rebecca Pritchard
A Nurse's Story: Medical Missionary in Korea and Siberia, 1915-1920 by Delia Battles Lewis

Visit us at: https://www.frayededgepress.com/

www.ingramcontent.com/pod-product-compliance
Lightning Source LLC
Chambersburg PA
CBHW071004080526
44587CB00015B/2337